DA **evenotes**

To Kevin
love

POMONA

A Pomona Book
POM:32
Published by Pomona Books 2019
Suite 4
Bridge House
13 Devonshire Street
Keighley
West Yorkshire
BD21 2BH

www.pomonauk.com

A CIP catalogue record for this book
is available from the British Library

ISBN: 978-1-904590-34-7

Set in Linotype Granjon by Geoff Read
Design: www.geoffread.com

Cover image of David Gedge and photos within the book
by Jessica McMillan

Made in England

Printed and bound by TJ International, England

CONTENTS

INTRODUCTION

I never wanted to be in a band.

What I mean by that is, I don't actually remember any point in my life where I specifically thought, 'I want to be a musician.' It's just kind of always been there. As a teenager I was constantly in groups of one ridiculous sort or another. Even before that, when I was off sick from school, I used to listen to Radio 1 all day, from 9am, until my parents got home from work. I have always been obsessed with records, and it might sound odd but I always knew that I'd be working in the music industry some day in one form or another.

For the most part I grew up in Middleton, near Rochdale. It's a suburb of Manchester but also a small town in its own right. After leaving school, I went to the University of Leeds to study mathematics. I'd always found maths to be fairly easy, even though many of my friends found it perplexing. I think I just have some kind of aptitude for it. I was trying to be sensible, I suppose, in wanting to have a back-up career in case the music didn't take off. But I think if The Wedding Present had not succeeded I'd still, even now, be in some sort of band. I won't make any bones about it – it's an obsession.

Before The Wedding Present, I had been the main songwriter in a group called The Lost Pandas. A couple of members of that band – specifically, Keith Gregory and I – went on to form The Wedding Present, but the groups sounded quite dissimilar to each other, really. They represented different eras, I guess. The sound of The Lost Pandas was more juvenile and the lyrics were kind of abstract. My writing technique was definitely still evolving.

The Lost Pandas imploded when a couple of the members decided to move to New York. Keith and I were determined to carry on, so we had to find new members. I roped in an old school friend of mine called Peter Solowka to play the guitar. At this point I also changed the name of the band to The Wedding Present.

Initially, we had great difficulty finding a drummer. We had about 10 during one year, in fact. When we finally met Shaun Charman he was the bassist in another band, and the only time he'd ever picked up drumsticks was when they'd swapped instruments during rehearsals for a laugh. But, to us, his personality and the music he liked were more important than his ability and so we decided that the fact that he couldn't actually play the drums wasn't necessarily an obstacle to him becoming the Wedding Present drummer.

Meeting Shaun was significant in the development of the band because he encouraged us to adopt a more punky and aggressive style of playing. That ferociousness, together with a certain discordance and edginess, has always been part of the Wedding Present sound but I'm also a big fan of pop music, too. I've never wanted our music to sound too 'sweet', though.

Most people in bands are about 17 or 18 when they release their first single, or at least they used to be. But I was 25 and Peter was even older, so we'd already had quite a few years of being in and around recording studios. I've known Peter since I was 11, and we had a band together while we were at school called Mitosis. I had already become used to being told that the guitars were too prominent in the mix or the vocals weren't quite right or the whole thing was far too loud. Those experiences definitely helped when we started recording as The Wedding Present. We were determined that this time we'd be doing it *our* way. In fact, for the first single, because we were paying for the studio time ourselves and it was only intended for release on our own label, we knew we could do whatever we wanted. We recorded it at a small studio in Headingley, Leeds, called The Billiard Room. As it turned out, the engineer, Carl Rosamond, totally understood what we were trying to do, anyway.

People have said that I sound a bit like Mark Burgess from The Chameleons on our early material, and I can only answer that by saying it's impossible to put into context how much of an influence that band had on me. I knew Mark and the two

3

guitarists, Dave Fielding and Reg Smithies, from school. Dave was actually one of my closest childhood friends and lived about five minutes' walk from our house. I always thought that he was this really cool kid. He was a brilliant musician, even when he was only 16. I'd go round to his house with my acoustic guitar and he'd be playing these amazing covers of Shadows songs through a tiny amplifier. And then he'd go on to tracks from a Yes album and play the parts as well as Steve Howe. When I was 16 I was thinking that I'd like to be a keyboard player because I was a fan of people like Keith Emerson and Rick Wakeman, but then punk came along and that was a massive cultural shift for me. I suddenly didn't want to play keyboards any more ... I wanted to play guitar in a band like The Jam or The Clash.

I used to go and watch Dave play with Reg in a group called Years and, at the same time, Mark play in his band, The Clichés. But then I left Middleton to go to Leeds University, and that's when the three of them formed The Chameleons. I thought The Chameleons were really great. I still do. They had amazing tunes and such a powerful sound. It's the kind of music that raises the hairs on your neck. I bought all their records, and Keith and I used to travel all over northern England to see them play live, along with my girlfriend at the time, Jaz Rigby. I clearly remember the night, in June 1981, when I first heard that The Chameleons had been invited to record a session for John Peel. He announced it at the end of a programme and that had such a huge impact on me – to realise that a band from little old Middleton could achieve something like that. On BBC Radio 1 no less. I was completely consumed by envy, of course, but it made me even more determined to do something with my own music.

So The Chameleons were almost bound to have had an influence on my songwriting until I found my own voice. They inspired The Lost Pandas more than The Wedding Present, though. When Shaun joined he actually said that he thought that we sounded too much like The Chameleons and, listening now to the first couple of Wedding Present singles, I can see why he would say that. But we did end up moving away from that style. Around that time I began to feel that The Wedding Present should have a personality of its own and so, if someone felt that a new song we were writing resembled another band, we'd try our best to not go down that route. There were a lot of people around at that time with a roughly similar sound to The Chameleons, bands like The Cure, Modern English and Echo And The Bunnymen. They used minor chords and effects and the singing was kind of affected. It might sound unlikely, but Altered Images were probably more of an influence on The Wedding Present! Their bass lines made a major melodic contribution to the arrangements and you can hear a similar thing happening in our songs. We also loved the Postcard Records bands like Josef K, and all the post-punk bands such as The Membranes and Bogshed. And there was always The Velvet Underground and The Fall, of course. But the point is that we didn't want to sound like we'd copied any of them.

THE WEDDING PRESENT

Go Out And Get 'Em, Boy!

I always felt that one of our other songs at the time – 'Will You Be Up There?' – was superior to 'Go Out And Get 'Em, Boy!', but we decided that 'Go Out And Get 'Em, Boy!' was more of a statement and, consequently, a better choice as a debut single. It had a real 'battle cry' feel to it. 'Will You Be Up There?', on the other hand, has never been released. So what do I know?

Shaun didn't feel quite confident enough on the drums to play on the recording of 'Go Out And Get 'Em, Boy!', though, so he asked his friend Julian Sowa to sit in for him. Our modus operandi at the time was to play everything at 100mph and Shaun isn't joking when he says that he was only able to play on the B-side, '(The Moment Before) Everything's Spoiled Again', because there was a slow bit in the middle where he was able to catch his breath.

There are about half a dozen different musical themes in 'Go Out And Get 'Em, Boy!' I remember a review saying that there were more ideas in that one song than some bands manage across an entire album. And, while I think it works on this track, an arrangement like that can often sound overwritten or too complicated. But it was our first single and, for all we knew, it might've been our last, so we wanted to pack it full of interesting ideas. We also intended for it to be an extreme record that leapt out of the radio and grabbed you by the ears, so we deliberately accentuated the thrashy guitars and frantic pace.

On this song, as with most of the others from that period, I'm doubling up on the strumming. So I'm playing both up strokes and down strokes. It can be quite difficult to do that at such high tempos but I think it's worth the effort because it holds everything together and really drives the song along. I have used that technique fairly extensively over the years even though it can be exhausting.

I'm a good rhythm guitarist; it's my forte. I'm definitely not a lead guitarist; I can't do complicated riffs or plucking. People have said in the studio, 'I can't believe you've sustained that strumming for so long and kept such good time', but it's how I've always played and it comes naturally to me. I treat the rhythm guitar almost like a percussion instrument. My sound is often so thin and jagged that it almost doesn't resemble a guitar any more because you can't hear the melody and the chords.

Our overall sound was 'dry'. We didn't want to use flangers or reverb pedals or echo units because everyone else seemed to be doing that in the 1980s. We wanted a more natural sound, to just plug into our amplifiers and play. I guess that was where the Velvet Underground influence comes in.

'Go Out And Get 'Em, Boy!' was written shortly after the Falklands War and is partly influenced by that conflict. Although I think there's passion in the lyric, the message is slightly unfocused and it's an approach that I moved away from after I'd decided to concentrate on a less 'poetic' style. My girlfriend after Jaz, Alexandra Duce, once told me she thought that my early lyrics were a bit pretentious, and that really hit me. There was this Lost Pandas song called 'Primacy' about waiting to cross at a pelican crossing. These days I'd think 'What a pompous title.' But at the time I suppose I liked it because it sounded like Joy Division. And the lyric went, 'Red man waiting for the green man,' after which I crowbarred in a reference to Native Americans! It was kind of gothy and set around those fashionable early 1980s minor chords. A lot of my early writing was of the 'Send me a flower, I'm going to die' school of lyricism.

I appreciated what Alex was saying, so I decided to try to write in a more conversational style instead of hiding behind imagery and deliberate ambiguity. Much of the Lost Pandas stuff was affected sixth-form poetry to be honest, which isn't that surprising because I'd only just left school. I've always admired writers who can make political statements work within the pop song format. Billy Bragg is a master of that, for example, but whenever I've tried I've always thought that it sounded clumsy and forced.

We set up our own label, Reception Records, to release 'Go Out And Get 'Em, Boy!' completely out of necessity. We'd sent out loads of demo tapes to labels and soon discovered that absolutely no one was interested in signing us. So we decided to save up and pay for the release ourselves. In doing so we essentially created our own record company. It was never an ambition to start a label – it came into being purely as a vehicle for The Wedding Present.

The Reception Records copies of 'Go Out And Get 'Em, Boy!' quickly sold out but, because we weren't yet a 'proper' organisation, the thought of re-pressing it didn't really cross our minds. Then a journalist called Neil Taylor interviewed the band for the *NME* and offered to re-release it on his label, City Slang (a different City Slang to the current one in Germany). We agreed. We were incredibly naïve. I think we said something along the lines of, 'OK, well, if you pay for lunch, you can release it.' I think we thought we were being cool rock stars. Red Rhino, who had distributed the first pressing, were appalled. They said, 'Why didn't you just ask us? We would have funded it.' And they were absolutely correct, of course. We'd let Neil re-release it without any contract or terms and conditions or anything.

Keith and I had assembled the first sleeve using a photograph we'd ripped out of a magazine and a packet of Letraset. The second sleeve was designed wholly by City Slang. We weren't consulted in any way. In fact, the first time I saw it was after Shaun had bought a copy from Jumbo Records in Leeds and brought it round to my house. We were both horrified. It was what I guess is called a 'wake-up call'. From that point we fiercely took control of all of our releases – the recordings, mixing, artwork, videos, everything – to the point where it became something of a fixation.

Hearing 'Go Out And Get 'Em, Boy!' being played on the John Peel show for the first time was genuinely one of the most exciting moments of my life. I'd spent my formative years listening to Peel to the extent of barely missing a single show. I'd first started in 1977 when a mate of mine at school told me that he'd been playing this amazing band called The Ramones. I taped pretty much every single Peel programme from the late 1970s until I went to live in Seattle in 2003. It was my musical universe and it undoubtedly shaped my personality, too. My principal ambition, for more than a few years, had been to have Peel air one of my songs on the radio and so, when he played the single, I was overjoyed. People often expect me to say that the highlight of being in The Wedding Present was appearing on *Top Of The Pops* or playing in Japan or whatever, but I don't think anything will ever surpass hearing that first play by John Peel.

Peel was, in some ways, too powerful, of course. He was massively influential and, obviously, his opinion was hugely respected but he was a bit like a Roman emperor in the Colosseum, deciding the fates of gladiators by moving his thumb up or down. I'm not saying he abused his position but he really did have the power to make or break a group. So we were very fortunate that he played our records. In the first few weeks after it came out he played 'Go Out And Get 'Em, Boy!' 10 times and that completely changed the situation we were in. It went from us going, 'Erm, can we play at your pub, please?' to people approaching us saying that they'd heard us on Peel, loved the record, and would we come and play at their venue in Carlisle.

My Favourite Dress

When we came round to making an album we decided that we didn't want to feature a lot of tracks that people had already heard. We didn't want to rip off the people who'd already bought the singles we'd released so far. So we waited until we had enough new songs for *George Best*. That's one of the reasons why it took so long to come out; it wasn't released until two and a half years after our first single.

During that time I came up with the idea for the LP title. I knew, as soon as I thought of it, that it was perfect and that there was no way that I was going to be talked out of it. Fortunately, the rest of the band thought it was a good idea, too. The words 'George' and 'Best' just somehow looked and sounded great to me. I'm also a Manchester United supporter so being able to put a picture of him on our sleeve made me happy, of course. I became a fan when I was growing up in Manchester, but my father is from Leeds and my mother is from Manchester so I have a fondness for both cities. This causes confusion in the football world (and especially with

13

Leeds-based Wedding Present fans) because of the bitter rivalry between the two Uniteds.

George Best was always something of an icon to me. I grew up in the 1960s and 1970s when he was the star of a brilliant team in a glamorous era. I'm not an authority on football by any means but anybody could see how naturally talented he was. I used to think he was the most entertaining player in the world. People like Pelé or Eusébio were obviously also super-human but George was always more unpredictable. He was a loose cannon waiting to go off. You never knew if he was going to nutmeg a defender or shout abuse at the referee.

We actually met George in 1987 when we did some photos with him around the time of the album release. I was completely terrified. Well, it's not every day you get to meet a living legend, is it? When our publicist Mick Houghton rang me to tell me that he'd successfully arranged the photo session I was stunned. I'd only agreed to the idea because I thought that there'd be no chance that George would agree to it. On the day I let our guitarist, Peter, do most of the talking because he was the more knowledgeable football fan. As well as feeling totally in awe, I felt a bit out of my depth. But George was extremely friendly and made us all feel relaxed. He actually seemed bemused. I mean, he obviously knew why we were there, but we didn't actually talk about music. We talked about his career and, somewhat unexpectedly, fishing! I made a faux pas as soon as he arrived, actually, because our manager had brought in a small crate of beer and I offered him a can. But this was at a time when he had some kind of an implant to help him fight his alcoholism. In my excitement and nervousness I'd genuinely forgotten that he had a drink problem, but he just laughed and said, 'No thanks, I'm on the wagon now.'

Using the name of such a famous person does have its drawbacks, of course. A journalist at the *NME* accused me of simply wanting to associate the name of my band with George Best forever – and I suppose there's a bit of truth in that – and when the record came out I did hear that some people thought it was an LP by George Best called 'The Wedding Present'. I don't care, though. Who wouldn't want to be associated with such a legend?

'My Favourite Dress' was always destined to be on *George Best* because we felt that it was our strongest song. We knew which songs we were going to release as singles before *George Best* but with 'My Favourite Dress' it felt like we had this 'ace in the hole' that we should probably save until the LP was ready.

I think it was Shaun who first said it was our best track, when he joined the group, so it was obviously around even in those early days. Initially, I didn't feel completely sure about it, but it soon became obvious through the reactions of people at concerts. In retrospect I can see why people felt that way about it. It's a pop song in the classic mould: simple, good melody, evocative words.

Lyrically, however, it's not really typical at all. The 'my favourite dress' line only comes right at the end when, usually, you find that songs have their lyrical base around the title. 'My Favourite Dress' is constructed so that the heartbreak increases throughout the song. You hear the story, which sets the scene, and then the climax comes when you visualise another man's hand on your girlfriend's dress. Then, once that has been revealed, there are no more words. There's just an instrumental end section. I wanted the lyric to finish like that. It's as if there's really nothing more to say.

Seeing another person's hand on the dress of the person I loved was a powerful image for me and it hurt a lot at the time. I can still feel that emotion now when I think about it and sing it. The song seems to have struck a chord with others as well. When people list their top five Wedding Present songs it's usually included. Fans have told me that the lyrics mean a lot to them because they're about things that they can empathise with: mundane fragments of life that carry a great deal of meaning. And those are feelings I have tried to encapsulate ever since moving away from the 'pretentious era' of the Lost Pandas lyrics. I now like to sing about people talking to each other, what they say and how they say it.

Still, I thought 'My Favourite Dress' was just another song. I am undoubtedly not a good critic of my own work. I don't always understand what makes certain songs more popular than others. There have been several times when I've thought, 'I've just written a really great song,' and everyone else has hated it. And vice versa. Not that I hated 'My Favourite Dress', I just saw it as one of the songs that we were playing in the set at the time that I quite liked.

I'm not totally happy with how *George Best* sounds when I listen to it now. The production is too thin. I think it's very representative of the era in which it was released – and I suppose that was the sound of the band in those days – but I just don't think it has stood the test of time as well as the other LPs. Partly because of that we re-recorded the whole album with Steve Albini, who worked on *Seamonsters* for us. Although I think the new version, *George Best 30*, sounds better than the original, it's still not totally there. It's probably because all the songs are so manic. They're played so quickly that there's no space for the instruments to breathe and we actually played them even faster on the re-recording. So it sounds more like a live album than an Albini album. He's a supremely talented engineer and I was interested to see where he'd go with it but I think those frantic arrangements just overpower anything anyone tries to do.

Interestingly, *George Best 30* features the band playing completely live in the studio and being recorded onto tape, whereas the original involved drum programming, sequencing and sampling. So, weirdly, the recording techniques used on the new version predate those on the 1987 one.

'Kennedy' is another prime example of me not being able to judge the quality of my own work. Are we seeing a theme? When it was being arranged I remember saying to the others, 'This one's got B-side written all over it.' I thought it was completely ordinary and kind of too simple, really. It had an obvious singalong quality but that didn't really appeal to me either; I just thought it was all too obvious. It was written when we were preparing tracks for *Bizarro* – which, by the way, is named after a Superman comic book character that I used to love – and I thought, at that time, that there was much better material around.

I also struggled with the lyric because I wanted to write a song that wasn't about relationships. I felt I needed to expand my range and do a song that was more metaphorical or something. So I came up with the idea of basing it loosely around the intrigue surrounding the assassination of President Kennedy. I'm not fond of the resulting lyric because it feels clichéd and built from slogans and that's something I usually shy away from. But I've always been interested in conspiracy theories and I'd just read a book called *The Gemstone File,* which went into various plots and assertions concerning the CIA and the Mafia. I did a substantial amount of research to explore all the ramifications, which is quite unusual for someone writing a pop song.

The apple pie line refers to a drug that was allegedly used by the CIA to induce heart attacks in people they wanted to liquidate. Apparently it smelt like apples and so they disguised it by putting it into pies. I've absolutely no idea how true that is. I also wanted to refer to the fact that the whole saga, including Jack Ruby's shooting of Lee Harvey Oswald, was televised. It felt like the first significant phenomenon of the TV age. The 'Harry' in the lyric refers to Aristotle Onassis, who went on to marry Jacqueline Kennedy, of course.

I really struggled to cram all the information I'd learnt into a lyric that didn't sound stupid. There were countless different drafts because I was continually chopping bits out and paring it down. It's the longest I have ever spent on a lyric; I was almost at the point of giving up, to be honest. But then I got to a stage where I decided that what I had would probably do, especially since I assumed it'd end up as the fourth track on an EP or something. And the rest is history. It's probably the song that people who aren't fans of the band know best. It's certainly the one that has been played most on the radio all around the world. I will say that it's an exciting song to play live, though.

I like the breakdown section with the bass and drums, but the long instrumental end section is my favourite part. I've always loved epic tracks like The Velvet Underground's 'What Goes On', which lasts for nearly nine minutes. Keith and I especially were big fans of that kind of repetition. But with 'Kennedy' we also wanted it to build in intensity as well, so we had all these extra layers come in and it gets bigger and more and more frantic as it goes on. I meticulously planned in advance how the overdubs would fit together because I've always hated the idea of wasting time in the studio working things out. I would write out arrangement sheets with the structures of the songs. I still do, in fact. It's also helpful for the engineer because they get to know in advance what's going to happen and when. So for the instrumental part of 'Kennedy' the arrangement sheet would have had it all broken down into sections, explaining when each part came in.

I don't see *Bizarro* as being a huge musical transition for us. There was more of a shift sonically after that. The difference between *George Best* and *Bizarro* was more to do with the fact that *George Best* is a bit flat, partly due to the songwriting and the lack of budget as well as our own inexperience. In a way I think *Bizarro* is kind of like a better version of *George Best*, with more dynamic changes in sound. We tried to include more texture and structure and variety on *Bizarro*. We wanted it to be more of an album, rather than just a collection of songs that were all played as fast as possible.

We did introduce some new ideas into The Wedding Present while we were working on *Bizarro,* though. Shaun had parted company with the band by then so we'd taken on a new drummer called Simon Smith who had an entirely different style. The drumming on 'Kennedy' is admired by everyone who hears it. We'd also just signed to RCA Records and so there were much larger budgets with which to play. This meant that *Bizarro* was recorded in The Wool Hall, near Bath – a fancy studio owned by Tears For Fears. It had a croquet court, which made us wonder why you'd pay £1,000 a day to play lawn games, but recording there did enable us to get the tracks closer to the sound that we'd imagined in our heads during the writing. I don't think we fully perfected that skill until the later albums, though. It has definitely been a gradual process.

I was absolutely blown away when I saw Steve Albini's band, Big Black, play in Leeds on their final tour in 1987. It was such a colossal sound, even though they didn't have a drummer. And then I heard his engineering on The Pixies' album *Surfer Rosa*. It sounded weird and interesting but still very natural. It was big and yet intimate and there was light and shade. I knew that The Wedding Present had all those things, too, but I wasn't hearing it in our records. So I thought we should work with Albini because he might help us to achieve that kind of texture.

RCA weren't really familiar with him but they agreed to set up a meeting, and we all got on well from the first moment. We tested the relationship in the studio by recording a couple of EPs and straight away the results sounded much more three-dimensional than the stuff we'd done on *George Best* and *Bizarro*.

So, at his suggestion, we went off to record *Seamonsters* at Pachyderm Disc, a studio in rural Minnesota with a vintage Neve mixing desk inside and three feet of snow outside. There wasn't a lot of talking about the music. There never is with Albini. There was a lot of talking about major record labels, though; he has a lot of views on that. When we signed to RCA they said, 'Now you've got all this money, you can spend as long as you want in the studio. You can experiment.' And on *Bizarro* we partly went along with that; we didn't really think that much about it. Albini reminded us that we didn't have to do that just because we could – we didn't have to spend a lot of time and money making records; we could simply go into the studio and thrash it out like we used to do in the days before *George Best*.

So we asked him how long we should book the studio for, because we'd taken six weeks to record *Bizarro*. He said, 'Six weeks? That's way too long. The Beatles recorded albums in a weekend and they sound great.' And we said, 'Yeah, but we're not The Beatles!' So I think we booked about a fortnight in the end and he said, 'OK, whatever.' We were finished in less than 12 days.

'Dalliance' was the first single off *Seamonsters* and it's one of my favourite Wedding Present songs. I think the way it builds is dramatic and exciting. I remember Keith saying that it felt like a series of explosions that get bigger and bigger. Even in the quiet bits there are these little drum fills or guitar parts that are continually bursting into life. Then you get to that huge jump in level for the instrumental section. And then it becomes even louder! I think Albini captured all that extraordinarily well and heightened the intensity.

Lyrically, the subject matter has nothing to do with me, making it different to most of my other songs. Jilly Cooper, the famous writer, was married to a publisher called Leo, who had been having an affair with another publisher called Sarah Johnson. I read a piece in *The Guardian* in 1990 by Sarah where she revealed that the affair had been going on for six years. She'd apparently been motivated to write the article by Jilly's habit of boasting in print about her 'perfect marriage'. Leo tried to defend himself by referring to the affair as 'a dalliance', but Sarah argued that it couldn't have been just a fling if it had lasted all that time. That struck me as a powerful argument to make, so I wrote the lyric from her point of view with the genders switched around.

It is an emotional and dark lyric, which suits the music. What struck me at the time was that because Jilly was so well known and liked, and because her husband had come back to her, all the articles were written from their point of view. Sarah's piece, on the other hand, seemed to be swimming against the tide of public opinion and that inspired me. I might have totally got the wrong end of the stick. I don't know. I don't think it matters, actually. Ultimately, it's a newspaper story that inspired a pop song. I have only done that kind of lyric – one where I'm writing a narrative about somebody else's life – a handful of times.

It was while we were writing the songs that would end up on *Seamonsters* that I started experimenting with a new tuning. I call a guitar with this particular tuning an 'E-guitar' because four of the six strings are tuned to an E note. Specifically, the A string is tuned down to an E and the D string is tuned up to an E. I discovered that a guitar tuned in this way had a really different sound because the chords are so odd. For example, you can play a D major with four F sharps in it. There's probably a name for that kind of chord. But the biggest advantage are the drones that you are able play on the bottom three strings, which are all tuned to E, remember. Stick a bottleneck over them and kick on a 1990s Yamaha overdrive pedal and it sounds like a massive siren. Somebody once compared it to the anguished cry of a beached whale. I used an E-guitar on every track of *Going, Going...* most recently, but it first appeared on *Seamonsters*. You can hear it on 'Dare', 'Lovenest', 'Corduroy' and, indeed, 'Dalliance'.

THE WEDDING PRESENT
Leicester Poly 5th May 1987   No.1

THE WEDDING PRESENT
Munchen Alabama-Halle
                                    No.2
                                    22/11/87

THE WEDDING PRESENT : LIVE TAPE NO.3
ROTTERDAM 30 MARCH 1988

THE WEDDING PRESENT : LIVE TAPE NO.4
VALENCIA 18 NOVEMBER 1988

ПЕРШИЙ ЗАПИС ІЗ КОНЦЕРТУ В ГРОМАДСЬКІЙ ЗАЛІ
МІДЛЕНДОУ, МАНЧЕСТЕР В НЕДІЛЮ 30-го КВІТНЯ 1989

THE WEDDING PRESENT : LIVE TAPE NO.6
FRANKFURT 3 NOVEMBER 1989

HOBOKEN   10 JUNE 1990

Come Play With Me
from The Hit Parade
by The Wedding Present
1992

Talking of guitars, I play an acoustic on the recording of 'Come Play With Me'. I'd used it previously on songs like 'Brassneck' and 'Crawl', but I've grown less and less fond of the sound of it over the years. I think they're fine as an overdub to add texture, but I don't think I'd ever use one as my main guitar now. I do remember loving the sound that My Bloody Valentine used to get out of an acoustic, though, so that probably inspired me.

I took the title 'Come Play With Me' from a film of the same name. It's a British 'sex comedy' from 1977. I've never actually seen it because I think it's almost certainly terrible, but that particular phrase seemed to suit the latter part of the lyric well. I enjoy lifting fragments from popular culture and re-using them in lyrics or titles. But I also like the way that a mundane moment in real life becomes more meaningful in a song. The story in 'Come Play With Me' is kind of obvious from the title but there is a twist. Leading up to the end section the song is about the culmination of a relationship, so the bulk of the lyric is a bit self-pitying. But then the narrator meets somebody else so the outro is this uplifting finale to follow all the anguish.

Paul Dorrington had replaced Peter as our guitarist by this point and he wrote the electric guitar parts. He always came up with great riffs, which is one of the reasons we'd asked him to join, of course. I tend to write my own bits – lyrics, vocal melodies, guitar lines – and other people write their parts. Paul was more interested in the American alternative rock bands of that time than Peter was, so I think he brought a different dynamic to the group. But he also had a huge knowledge of pop culture, so it was an interesting combination. He was as happy to do a Monkees cover version as he was coming up with a guitar part that sounded like The Jesus Lizard.

I encourage people in the band to put forward ideas for songs because even if I don't think it works, others might. Also, of course, there's always the chance that I will grow to like it eventually. I'll go away, maybe sleep on it, and then possibly change my mind. Things like that can move the group forward so I'm always open for band members to stamp their identity on our sound. That's why The Wedding Present have made this series of records that each have their own personality; it's because there have usually been different people playing on each one. I genuinely feel like I've been in about half a dozen bands. I have always said that the sound of The Wedding Present is the combined sound of the four people who are in the group at any given time.

I'm probably the opposite of Mark E. Smith in that I don't tell people what to do. In fact, I'd rather know what *they* want to do without my direction. I try to credit other band members properly. I always have done. In the early days the records only attributed 'Gedge' as the writer but that was just because I was the only member of the Performing Rights Society. So I would collect any royalties and then share them out.

'Come Play With Me' is officially our greatest hit. Well, so far, anyway! It is the only time The Wedding Present have ever graced the top 10. The reason for this is because it was part of the monthly *Hit Parade* project, which was the series of 12 limited-edition 7" singles that we released in 1992. RCA pressed 15,000 of each record with plans to sell 10,000 in the UK and save 5,000 for the rest of the world. But after the first couple of releases had sold out in a matter of days they realised that they'd underestimated the popularity of the series and asked for our permission to increase the numbers they were pressing. We wouldn't let them because we thought it would be unfair on people who were coming late to the project and were trying to collect them all. They would have less chance of getting hold of the early ones. So, instead, they decided to retain all 15,000 copies of the subsequent singles for sale in the UK. By the time 'Come Play With Me' was released, we were in this position where we were selling all 15,000 singles in the UK in two or three days. Added to that you have the fact that this single was released in the early May bank holiday week. So, while our singles were being snapped up in a couple of days all the other artists' sales were spread out over a week.

And when you took away a day of their sales because of the bank holiday it decreased their numbers by a percentage.

The promotional video for 'Come Play With Me' was also better-looking than many of the others, so maybe it was shown more. There was no way that RCA was going to pay for a dozen professional films so we just threw it open to anybody and everybody in the form of a news item in the music press. 'Do you think you can make a video for The Wedding Present for under £1,000? Well, get in touch!' We ended up with a couple of bin liners full of VHS tapes sent in by hopeful filmmakers. But Jeremy Hibbard, the person who made the video for 'Come Play With Me', worked for the BBC in Leeds so he had access to better equipment and skilled personnel.

We didn't appear on *Top Of The Pops* every month. I think we possibly might have been invited most months but, for example, on one occasion we were in America. And there were a couple of other times when we physically just couldn't make it. Then, later, we actually turned a couple down, which probably shocked RCA's promotions department. I think it just felt a bit weird, because the record would come out on a Tuesday and be sold out by the Thursday and then be in the following week's charts. So we would be playing on *Top Of The Pops* the next Thursday, after the single had been unavailable for a week. It all just felt a little pointless. I think maybe the novelty wore off, too. In retrospect I do regret that to a certain extent, because it would have been great to have been on *Top Of The Pops* a few more times. I suppose I didn't realise that our association with it, and even the remaining life of the programme itself, would be so short. You kind of assumed it was an institution that would be around forever. I'd loved the programme as a kid – and then as a teenager – and I think that we only ended up going on it about three or four times in total.

It was Keith who had come up with the initial idea for the *Hit Parade* project. He just happened to mention at a rehearsal that the American record company Sub Pop had been doing a series of 7"s called *The Singles Club* and how he thought it'd be cool if we could do that. It was one of those ideas where you immediately thought, 'Now I've heard that, we have got to do it.' Five minutes later, we'd agreed on all the specifics. We would do an original on each A-side and a cover on each B-side. All the record sleeves would match and feature famous versions of the numbers 1 to 12. We'd make a video and a T-shirt for each one, too. Even the record middles would form a comic book-style story of their own, drawn by Paul. The hardest part was trying to convince RCA but, to their credit, they agreed.

We thought it'd be nice to have a different session and producer for each single, but recording just two songs every month was out of the question, both from a logistical and an economic point of view. So we grouped them into quarters. We recorded six tracks in four distinct sessions and used different producers each time. So it kind of had a seasonal feel. It would have been more sensible to have had the songs pre-written, I guess, but that seemed to be at odds with the spirit of the project. So we would write three songs, arrange three cover versions, toddle off into the studio, record them, mix them, film three videos, print three T-shirts ... and then the process would start all over again. Logistically, I've got to say, it was a complete nightmare to organise.

The first producer was Chris Nagle, who had recorded a lot of Manchester bands, including Joy Division. The next was Ian Broudie, from The Lightning Seeds, who I think brought the pop sheen to our sound that you can hear on 'Come Play With Me'. Then came Jimmy Miller, the famous Rolling Stones producer. Finally, there was Brian Paulson, an American producer who was something of an Albini protégé. The remarkable thing was that they were all completely different; some got way more involved than others. We hardly saw Jimmy Miller towards the end of his session, if I'm honest. He'd pop down from his room, listen to a track, shake a tambourine and then disappear again.

I really enjoyed doing *The Hit Parade*. It was quite stressful at times because we were working to deadlines. We'd be saying, 'It's the end of the quarter and the tracks aren't ready to record yet!' But I don't think the songs suffered as a result of having been written to order. I'm really proud of all those A-sides. I'm not quite as happy with all of the cover versions but overall it was a positive experience and we learnt a lot. Ultimately, I think the biggest problem I had with it was that it became so media-friendly. Commentators would focus on the uniqueness of the project or the fact we ended up in *The Guinness Book Of*

Records or how it was some kind of bizarre investigation into the decline of the record industry. Occasionally, you'd feel like saying, 'You know, we are releasing some pretty good songs here, too.'

THE WEDDING PRESENT · THE BBC SESSIONS · DEI8411-2

THE WEDDING PRESENT · EVENING SESSIONS 1986-1994 · STRANGE FRUIT · SFRSCD029

THE WEDDING PRESENT · PEEL SESSIONS 1987-90 · STRANGE FRUIT/DUTCH EAST · DEI8126-2

THE WEDDING PRESENT
THE COMPLETE
PEEL SESSIONS

BBC

The Wedding Present · Marc Riley Sessions Volume 1 · Hatch Records · HAT14CD

The Wedding Present · Marc Riley Sessions Volume 2 · Hatch Records · HAT19CD

The Wedding Present · Marc Riley Sessions Volume 3 · Hatch Records · HAT24CD

THE WEDDING PRESENT

TOMMY

THE WEDDING PRESENT

BIZARRO

THE WEDDING PRESENT

SEAMONSTERS

THE WEDDING PRESENT

THE HIT PARADE

THE WEDDING PRESENT

WATUSI

THE WEDDING PRESENT

MINI

THE WEDDING PRESENT

SATURNALIA

The Wedding Present
The Complete Ukrainian John Peel Sessions

HAT30CD/DVD

Following the release of the final *Hit Parade* single, Keith left the band. That was a significant moment for me. It really felt like I was losing someone crucial to the group, and I was apprehensive about how we'd continue. More than just a friend, Keith had been the co-founder of The Wedding Present and my staunch ally from those Lost Pandas days, and I relied heavily on his guidance. If there was ever such a thing as a constitution on how The Wedding Present is run, we wrote it together. He'd actually tried to leave a couple of times before, but on each occasion I'd talked him into staying. Nonetheless, when you're in possession of something you hold as dearly as I do with this band, I suppose you just make it work, whatever hand you've been dealt.

If Keith's leaving wasn't enough in itself to trigger a re-evaluation, at the same time we also parted company with RCA Records and signed a new deal with Island Records. We'd had a genuinely good working relationship with RCA through *Bizarro, Seamonsters* and *The Hit Parade* but it felt like it was time to go. The turnover of staff at major record labels in those days was swift, and literally all the people who had been there when we'd signed in 1988 had gone by 1993. New people who, quite understandably, were championing their own, more recent, signings had replaced them.

When Korda Marshall left RCA we lost our biggest supporter at the company. We were assigned a new A & R person. He was nice enough, but he just didn't have that love and understanding of The Wedding Present or the drive to make it work within the major label system, so we kind of saw the split coming.

Island initially seemed like it would be a good fit for the group, but we signed to Island in the USA rather than Island in the UK. At first we didn't think it would matter, but the band was significantly more successful and active at home than it was in North America, so the UK was obviously the focus for us and the label. Consequently, we were dealing with the Island people in London, who didn't really know who we were or the philosophy behind The Wedding Present. We'd sort of been foisted on them, if you like, as this new signing to the American label. And this was all before the age of email, of course, so communication wasn't as easy as it would have been nowadays. Creatively, we were signed to the right label, but life at RCA had been considerably more straightforward.

Our A & R person at Island, Jesse Obstbaum, recommended a producer from Seattle called Steve Fisk, who had apparently made his name working with pretty much every famous band that had ever come out of Seattle. I didn't know a lot about Steve and initially, on the face of it, he might not have seemed like an obvious choice. But we'd also started to think, around that time, that we wanted to modify the sound of the band again. Up until then The Wedding Present had been, pretty much, a guitar-based indie-rock band in the generic sense. But we had now reached a point where we wanted to experiment with other instruments ... like pianos, organs or brass. Steve was also the keyboard player from the low-fi pop groups Pell Mell and Pigeonhed and his knowledge of vintage keyboards like Mellotrons and Farfisas is immense. I think that made up our minds, so off we went to Seattle to record *Watusi*. Keith had been replaced on the bass by Darren Belk who was well up for joining the search for our new 'old' sound, especially when it came to attempting surf instrumentals and the like. I even convinced him to sing the lead vocal on 'Shake It'.

We wrote and arranged the songs for the *Watusi* sessions in the usual way but in the back of our minds we had vague plans for recording alternate takes to use as B-sides for singles. We were thinking of the usual acoustic versions – basically recording them with acoustic guitars, drums played with brushes, stuff like that – but working with Steve turned that plan on its head. We ended up preferring the alternate versions and so we put them on the album instead. All that helped to make *Watusi* feel very different from our earlier LPs.

One of the instruments Steve introduced me to was the Optigan. It was made by a subsidiary of the toy manufacturer Mattel in the early 1970s and got its name because the noise it made came from pre-recorded 'optical' soundtracks that came on discs. It had such a beautiful, haunting sound that we immediately wanted to experiment with it, and we had this song called 'Spangle' that seemed like the obvious choice. I think that was probably the very moment when Cinerama – my soon to be 'other band' – was born. But more of that later.

For 'Click Click' Paul used a variant of what's called an 'Open D5' guitar tuning – where most of the strings are tuned to either D or A to make the riff ring out – while Darren and I are droning on D notes underneath. I think the overall sound is quite hypnotic but it doesn't become completely dream-like because there are still lots of little dynamic lifts as the track progresses.

Running parallel to all the instrument changes we wanted to try on the album, I also had a growing desire to experiment with some more sophisticated vocal arrangements and 'Click Click' is the best example of how that materialised. For The Wedding Present to try something like this was unprecedented. Heather Lewis from Beat Happening and Carrie Akre from Hammerbox were drafted in by Steve to help with the singing. It's a song that always goes down very well live. People love the a cappella ending, but being one of just three voices in a room of a thousand people who're all listening to you intently can be terrifying.

Watusi was our only LP for Island. We'd signed a three-album deal, but the label was taken over by Polygram quite soon after we'd released the LP. Jesse was sacked, along with a few other people. At the same time they culled some artists from their roster, too, including us. So, perhaps inevitably, after the first pressing of *Watusi* sold out, it wasn't repressed. It hasn't been available on vinyl since the mid-1990s. And, until Edsel Records released it on CD in 2014, it hadn't been available in any physical form whatsoever. So I call it, rather melodramatically, The Wedding Present's 'lost' album.

Departing from Island didn't really concern us too much because, as I say, we'd kind of fallen into this UK/USA divide. After leaving both Island and RCA we were able to deal with the change pretty easily. The Wedding Present has always had a strong sense of independence, regardless of which label we're on. We run the band and the label sells the records. Some musicians, quite understandably, don't want to be bothered with all the business. They just want to focus on writing the songs and making the records so if they find themselves without the support of a label, they can flounder. But we've always been interested in the business side. I remember a lawyer at RCA being impressed that we ran such 'a tight ship'.

THE WEDDING PRESENT · BRASSNECK

THE WEDDING PRESENT SONGS

dalliance

THE WEDDINGPRESENT

RCA

BMG

PKA4495

THE WEDDING PRESENT

PRCS 0870-1

the wedding present

the wedding present

it's a gas

THE WEDDING PRESENT

THE BBC SESSIONS

DEDK411-4

WEDDING PRESENT

GEORGE BEST

LEEDS

Go, Man, Go

In 1995 we signed to Cooking Vinyl Records, who were a big independent label at the time. The deal they offered us was something we hadn't encountered before. They wanted us to release the usual LP but precede it with a mini album. I don't know why they suggested that but I'm guessing it was something to do with 're-launching' the band. Anyway, we thought it was a cool idea, something different and I remember thinking, 'We could do another 10"!' I've always loved 10" records, since the days of playing my parents' shellac singles when I was a kid. So we agreed. Because it was only going to be six songs, I decided to make a theme out of it. Darren, who by this point had now moved to guitar following the departure of Paul, was an ex-mechanic and interested in cars, so I thought we could make it a concept album loosely based on driving and call it *Mini*. He took photos of an actual 1968 Austin Mini Countryman for the sleeve that we ended up buying and using as a raffle prize. John Peel drew the winner live on Radio 1 and I drove the car down to Wales to present it myself.

Other people had already used 'Go, Man, Go' as a title by the time I got around to it. It was the name of a film from 1954 about the Harlem Globetrotters and also a British pop music radio show, again from the 1950s. But I saw it on a postcard that featured the cover of a pulp novel about hot-rod drivers. I just thought it sounded like a hipster phrase. The lyrics are very direct, classic 'me', I suppose. It's a straightforward break-up song. There's often nothing to look for in my lyrics. I don't hide much. That's just my style, and I've honed it over the years.

'Go, Man, Go' is only a couple of minutes long but it packs a heck of a lot into that little space, which is one of the reasons why I like it. The wistful vocal and solo acoustic guitar introduction quickly transforms into chunky electric guitars and a soaring bass line. It also contains one of my favourite vocal melodies. I love Darren's guitar line, too. It isn't overplayed; he stops it before it becomes too ostentatious. I think that's very typical Wedding Present in many respects – the music is often quite subtle, in that it is as much about what we don't play and what listeners fill in with their imagination. And I've never liked guitar solos. Darren was good at that kind of musical understatement. He also contributed to many of the songs on *Saturnalia*, which was the 'proper' album for Cooking Vinyl, but he ended up leaving the group after the recording of *Mini*.

People do that. They join the group because they think it will be brilliant and that they will be writing songs and making records and travelling the world for a living, and it will all be fabulously exciting. And, don't get me wrong, it is. But it's also hard work and it can be stressful, particularly when you're away from home for ridiculously long periods of time. You go to Austria or somewhere for the first time and it's fantastic. The second time, yeah, here we are again in Austria; it's great. But by the time of your third or fourth visit you've been there already and you maybe want to go to places where the band is possibly never going to play. It can also create tension in people's lives and with their relationships. You'll be just going to bed in Los Angeles, all excited after playing the Whisky a Go Go, while, at that very same moment, your girlfriend will be getting up for work on a freezing, dark morning back in Yorkshire to pay your mortgage. I am not saying that's what happened with Darren, but I have seen things like that causing problems. You can lose contact with your friends and family pretty easily. I think that's one of the reasons nobody with kids has ever been in the group, though several have had children after they left.

I can usually see it coming to be honest. People will start turning up to rehearsals maybe a little less prepared than they used to. Or arguments will crop up that wouldn't have in the past. Everything becomes a pain for them. 'What? We have to leave at 7am?' 'Yes, it's the only flight that's available.' You start to realise that they don't really want to be in the room, even if they don't fully recognise it themselves. That's just the way it is. Some people stay for 12 years and some people stay for 12 months. I think people possibly suppress their personality a bit in order to fit in with the band at first, but then, over time, it will start to niggle them. I have had several conversations over the years with people who I've noticed are just not enjoying it any more. I've told them that it's fine if they want to leave but, if they want to stay, they need to buck up and stop making it difficult for other people. I always have to look at the big picture. The band has to come first. Sometimes that has worked and other times they have just left. I really hate those conversations. Having to ask people to leave the group is by far the worst part of my job because I hate confrontation. As a result I have often found myself putting up with unreasonable behaviour for longer than I should have. But then I've been criticised for that, too. I've definitely been guilty of being aware that I need to ask people to leave but have papered over the cracks because it meant that we could get the album recorded or the tour finished.

There has often been a fragile balance of personalities within the group. People from completely different backgrounds have to live, travel and work together in intense situations. You'll have band members with different ages, gender and talent ... all contributing to The Wedding Present with varying and ever-changing amounts of enthusiasm.

But people always want to be in this band, so it has never been difficult to find new musicians. It's usually done by word of mouth, followed by auditions. Only once has somebody sent me an actual CV in advance to keep on file and use if a position opens up, but people are always saying to me, 'If you ever need a drummer or whatever, I'd kill to be in The Wedding Present.' That's actually what Andy Burnham, the mayor of Greater Manchester, said but I think he was joking.

At the point when Darren left we were in the middle of writing the songs that we'd be using for the promised, but as yet untitled, full-length album for Cooking Vinyl. The new guitarist, Simon Cleave, came in with riffs that we immediately used on new songs called 'Montreal' and '2, 3, Go'. I thought they were both brilliant and the group seemed re-energised once again. We finished writing the rest of the songs and went off to record the album at September Sound – a studio on the banks of the River Thames owned by The Cocteau Twins. I have always been a massive fan of that band so it was amazing to meet the guitarist, Robin Guthrie. I remember that we chatted on the roof of the studio about The Sex Pistols – he was off to see them at a festival or something – but our conversation was interrupted when we saw a passer-by being hit by lightning on the road outside the studio. They weren't seriously hurt, but it did make us think that being on the roof during a storm probably wasn't the best idea in the world! Robin mentioned that I could pop downstairs and meet the Cocteau's singer Elizabeth Fraser but I was more nervous of that than by being hit by lightning!

Both of those first two Cleave songs were released as singles. What a great way to announce your arrival in a band. Also around that time, Jayne Lockey became the new bass player. She'd already provided some singing on *Mini,* including 'Convertible', which had been the first Wedding Present duet. 'Montreal' is a pop song but, melodically, it's kind of off-kilter. Simon used the same 'D' guitar tuning that Paul had used on 'Click Click'. The vocals on it are louder than some of the other tracks, I think, because of the nature of the arrangement. It reminds me of a Go-Betweens song with its piano and the fact that it isn't really rocky. The lyric is about that feeling where you are expecting something and you assume it will come along, and then you realise that it isn't going to, and it's shocking. Montreal was just a place I used because I liked the word and I love the city.

Saturnalia is noteworthy because it's kind of experimental. Both Simon and Jayne had previously been in a band called Tse Tse Fly, which was an avant-garde alternative rock group. It felt like they were importing some unconventional ideas into The Wedding Present. Having said that, Tse Tse Fly weren't particularly what you'd call tuneful, but *Saturnalia* is one of our most melodic LPs. I especially love Jayne's singing on 'Montreal' because it's so haunting and really captures the mood. I can remember when she first heard the lyric. She said, 'Aww, that's so sad.'

The song still affects me because it is a particularly melancholy story. I am obsessed with the nature of relationships, and one aspect of it – the surprise and the shock of one ending unexpectedly – is a major part of that. I don't think 'Montreal' is a bitter song, though. It feels more resigned than anything. Sometimes in a relationship a person will hide their dissatisfaction and so it'll come as a shock to their partner when they choose to end it.

I suppose I'm quite heartless in that I don't worry too much about how the real-life people who have inspired my lyrics will feel about being in a song. Having said that, I sometimes get pangs of guilt because, in a way, I am using them. But then most of the time people fail to recognise themselves anyway. I have talked to people about songs that have been written about them and they have heard it and not even noticed. And then you'll get other people who have thought that songs were about them when they're not. I think it shows how people can have a different perception of themselves. People will say that they would never do something that the protagonist in a lyric did, when, in fact, they have done that very thing. No one wants to feel like they're a bad person.

People ask me, 'Are all these songs about you?' And I think the answer is yes, they kind of are. Some are obviously more autobiographical than others and some of them are completely made up. But they're still all about me, ultimately. I become totally immersed with a lyric, and I try to make it as personal as possible by writing about what I know. If a story is made up, I've just projected myself into that particular situation. I imagine it's a bit like method acting. I used to say in interviews, 'No, no, they're not all about me; there are maybe three that are and then the rest are fictional.' But – and here's your exclusive – they all are, really.

Relationships are a massive subject, and they mean so much to people – it's the thing that binds us together as humans, the way we relate to each other and speak to each other. I've never had writer's block because I've always been able to find something to write about. One person can say one sentence and there will be enough there to inspire a song. It's because of the effect of that one simple string of words. It'll impact upon somebody else, and there'll be an observer's point of view and the original writer's point of view. I feel like I've only scratched the surface of the subject.

In 2017 we released an EP called *The Home Internationals,* which was completely instrumental. I loved doing that, partly because I didn't have to think about writing lyrics. I put a ton of effort into the words. Sometimes I'll spend a day on a lyric and then throw it away because I'm unhappy with it. Days like that are disheartening, but I'm obsessive about maintaining a certain standard. So to be freed of the need to create a lyrical narrative for a while was refreshing. I know some people aren't fond of instrumentals because they like to hear a story in the music. I remember talking to my friend Clare Wadd from Sarah Records about it and she said, 'But I just like a song.' For her, I guess, an instrumental is merely a piece of music where the words haven't been written yet. I can appreciate that. I also find that without a singing part to lead the arrangement you feel obliged to replace the vocal melody with tunes on the instruments, which can take you off on different tangents. I did enjoy working on those instrumentals, so I might do more of that.

Sometimes I think I should probably just move into a totally different lyrical field. That might open up a can of worms, though, where I have to go through the process of getting comfortable writing about a whole new subject.

TONE CD 003

TONE CD 003

TONE CD 005

TONE CD 007

TONE CD 008 CINERAMA health and efficiency

MFO 42403

MFO 42403

TONE CD 010 CINERAMA before it melts

TONE CD 012 CINERAMA success

TONE CD 016 CINERAMA don't touch that dial

MFO 42405-PRO and when she was bad from the album Torino

CINERAMA

CINERAMA | LOLLOBRIGIDA

CINERAMA | YOUR CHARMS

CINERAMA SUPERMAN

CINERAMA health and efficiency

CINERAMA health and efficiency

VR VR VOOM

MANIFESTO

MANIFESTO

MANIFESTO

CINERAMA

VALENTINA CINERAMA TONE CD 052

T.W.70 42404 I CINERAMA TORINO

cinerama   this is cinerama   manifesto   COCK CD 180

TONE CD 05   CINERAMA   CINERAMA HOLIDAY

CINERAMA   SEVEN WONDERS OF THE WORLD   TONE CD 051

CINERAMA
THE COMPLETE PEEL SESSIONS

Hard, Fast And Beautiful

The basic idea behind Cinerama was that I wanted to make music that sounded filmic but also to reference the classic pop records I'd grown up listening to in the 1960s. In particular, I wanted 'Hard, Fast And Beautiful' to sound like it was from the soundtrack of a French movie from the 1970s, so I based it around an evocative piano part with a backdrop of strings. But then there's also a huge singalong pop chorus. I stole the title from a 1950s film about tennis, but it doesn't have anything to do with the lyric.

I have always loved film music. I've been a fan of John Barry and Ennio Morricone for as long as I can remember. Even though we went down the alternative guitar path with The Wedding Present, I'd always yearned to do some music like this. I think *Watusi* gave me the belief that I could successfully deviate from the norm, so when The Wedding Present took a break in 1997 I decided to give it a go.

For the recording of the *Va Va Voom* album, I used session musicians. I played guitar and sang as usual, but most of the music on that record was performed by people who I'd never previously met. When they came into the studio they were hearing the songs for the first time. The drummer, bass player and guitarist all came up with their own parts on the spot, under my direction, in the studio. I wrote the keyboard parts, string arrangements and brass and flute parts at home on the computer. I can't begin to explain how different a way of working this was for me, and it took me a while to get my head round it.

During the mid-1990s using computers to assist in the making of music had become much more accessible to someone like me who has no sound engineering knowledge. By that I mean that they plummeted in price and became considerably more user-friendly. With the aid of some basic sequencing software and an Akai sampler I was able to record demos of the early Cinerama songs onto a digital eight-track recorder synched to my computer using drum loops, a keyboard, a microphone and my guitars. But, despite all the machinery I was using to write the songs, I still wanted Cinerama to sound like 'a band' and not just a drum machine and keyboards, so that's why I decided to use session musicians for the studio recordings. The software enabled me to print out scores for people like the strings players, so, again – even though I can't score music – I was able to explain by and large what I wanted from the musicians.

Dare Mason was the producer and engineer on *Va Va Voom* and he was very helpful in sourcing some extremely talented musicians, like Marty Willson-Piper from The Church who brought half a dozen amazing guitars into the studio with him. For all my previous records I'd been in a band and all the songs had been written, arranged and rehearsed a long time before we'd even set foot in the recording studio. The *Va Va Voom* sessions were much more fluid. Sometimes the session musicians would play it completely as I'd written it and sometimes they would say, 'Well, I can see what you're trying to do but the flute part would sound better if I did it like this.'

There was actually an amusing moment during the recording of 'Hard, Fast And Beautiful' when we had the pianist in. I had a strong idea of how I wanted the part to be, but I can't play the piano, so I had to write the piece, bit by bit, on the computer. I would record a few seconds of the right-hand part and then a few seconds of the left. And then I would move on to the next section. It was a convoluted process with lots of overdubs – adding bits here and there – but when I was finally happy with it I printed out the score and brought it proudly along to the studio we were using to record piano. The pianist was a friend of Dare's called Davey Ray Moor, but what I didn't know was that he was a hugely talented composer and multi-instrumentalist. He took one look at my score and said, 'I can't play this.' I asked, 'Why not?', thinking that maybe we'd need someone with greater skills. He laughed and said, 'Because the way it's currently written I would literally need to have three hands.'

One of the more stressful moments of the *Va Va Voom* recording sessions was during the recording of the female vocal parts. For a couple of the songs I asked one of my favourite singers, Emma Pollock from The Delgados, if she wanted to make a guest appearance. She agreed and promptly flew down from Scotland to join me in Dare's studio in London. She knocked out a couple of brilliant vocal parts very quickly and her voice sounded amazing. But for the rest of the album I had coerced my girlfriend Sally Murrell into singing. Sally wasn't a musician and had no experience of being in – or even the vaguest desire to be in – a band, but I thought that with a few singing lessons she'd be fine. And she was, eventually. Her vocals on the finished record are fantastic. But trying to cajole a good performance out of somebody with zero studio experience proved to be much tougher than I'd imagined. To be fair, Dare wasn't the most sympathetic of producers. He'd turn off the talkback while Sally was at the microphone and say, 'David, this just isn't working.' That made me feel guilty and pressured. He eventually persuaded me to try one of his friends, a professional singer called Faith, in an effort to save time and get the project back on track. Sally was, inevitably, very upset and I felt blameworthy for having forced her into this situation and then removing her from it. I have horrible memories of a tearful meal in Hammersmith. But the next day, when Faith auditioned, both Dare and I knew instantaneously that she didn't have the right-sounding voice for the arrangements. She was from more of a folk music background. It took me a while to persuade both Dare and Sally to give plan A another go but when we did it was like we were working with a different person. I don't know if it was because of Faith's failure or Sally's getting used to being in the goldfish bowl of the studio, but her performance during the second attempt was much improved. She'd always had a great tone but she was now singing much more in tune and in time.

Va Va Voom was, for better or worse, the only project I've ever been involved with where I've done exactly what I wanted to do throughout. That never really happened in The Wedding Present because in a band you're always making compromises. It's a team effort. I did feel lonely at times, assembling everything together on my own at home, but I did enjoy the control.

The reaction to Cinerama from Wedding Present fans was 50-50. Some people found it an interesting change, like when we'd recorded Ukrainian folk music for Peel sessions in the late 1980s, whereas others were saying, 'What is this rubbish?' For me it was fundamentally a chance to explore a totally different way of working. But when I listen back to *Va Va Voom* now I really enjoy it because I'm proud of the arrangements and I love the sound of that record, not just because I put my heart and soul into it.

CINERAM

HE GIRL FROM THE DDR (

Va Va Voom was a real solo album, but I released it as the first LP by Cinerama because I didn't want to put it out under the name of David Gedge. I suppose I was still trying to give the impression that a band had recorded it – or a mini-orchestra, actually – even though there wasn't one. And calling it The David Gedge Band or something would really not have been my style. In retrospect it was quite a serious marketing mistake. I still meet people today who have only just realised that Cinerama is me. They say, 'I wish you'd have put 'Featuring David Gedge from The Wedding Present' on a sticker on the front of the record so that I could have heard it when it came out.' But, again, I wouldn't have been comfortable doing that, even though Cooking Vinyl, who released *Va Va Voom,* suggested it at the time.

So, I had no actual band but when the album came out I wanted Cinerama to play live. This was the summer of 1998 and the previous Wedding Present concerts had been 18 months earlier, so I was missing the live experience. I was also proud of an album that I'd spent such a long time working on, and I wanted to play the songs to people. I contacted the members of The Wedding Present who'd recorded *Saturnalia,* but only Simon Cleave out of that line-up was interested in playing with Cinerama. Some of the people who had played on the recordings of *Va Va Voom* were happy to reprise their role on stage but many, like the bassist Anthony Coote, had other commitments. He was also the bass player in the Abba tribute band Bjorn Again, who were just about to appear at the Royal Albert Hall. So it's not surprising that he didn't want to join us for little gigs in tiny venues across the country. Fortunately, he did recommend his friend Terry de Castro, whose own band, Goya Dress, had just split up. So Terry joined Cinerama and has played music with me off and on ever since.

I enjoyed working with Simon and Terry during those early Cinerama years. I'm not saying it was easy. In fact, it was extremely stressful. Cinerama wasn't anywhere near as commercially successful as The Wedding Present had been but, because of the complicated song arrangements and the need for additional musicians, it was much more costly to finance. Writing, arranging, recording, mixing, playing live; everything cost more. The figures didn't balance and, consequently, everything had to be done on the tiniest of budgets. I ended up investing all of my savings into the band because that was the only way I could keep it going. I remember having a meeting with Cooking Vinyl where I was adamant that Cinerama could actually be bigger than The

Wedding Present because it had a more commercial sound, and they were telling me that no solo record ever sells more than the artist's group's records. They were totally right.

It was a struggle but it was exciting to be back in a band again and one that was different than The Wedding Present. So I decided to press on with writing a second Cinerama album. I'd fulfilled my contractual obligations with Cooking Vinyl by this point, so I also decided to start my own label again. I called it Scopitones after the Scopitone machine (a 16mm forerunner of the video jukebox invented in France in the 1950s) and started planning the recording of the next album, *Disco Volante,* which I named after the villain's boat in the Bond film *Thunderball.*

Now that Simon Cleave was playing guitar with me again, the next batch of songs was created in partnership with him. I was still writing the orchestration and keyboard parts on the computer, but the new songs inevitably became more guitar orientated. In some ways we were writing in a way that was half Wedding Present, half Cinerama. I would drive over to Cologne in Germany – where he lives – with my car dangerously loaded up with gear: musical instruments, desktop computer, sampler, mixing desk and digital eight-track recorder. We'd basically set up a makeshift studio in his living room. The flat he lived in was near a church, and I loved the sound of the bells, so we decided to record them. They sounded very 'spaghetti western' (Simon loves Morricone, too) and we ended up using them on the extended version of a song called 'Quick, Before It Melts'.

You can hear how 'Wow' is much more guitar driven than the tracks on *Va Va Voom*. It's also one of those songs that builds and builds. It's actually a bit like 'Kennedy' in a way but instead of guitars the layers are strings and other orchestration. I decided to go back to working with Steve Albini for *Disco Volante,* and I think that gave the recordings a darker feel. We did the guitars, bass and drums in Albini's Chicago studio and then finished it all off in England with Dare. If you remove the orchestration, I think 'Wow' could easily be mistaken for a Wedding Present song and because of that it probably brought some people who were not massive fans of the earlier Cinerama stuff back into the fold.

'Wow' contains many of my favourite sounds: those immense Albini drums, Simon's twangy guitar, Sally's evocative vocals, haunting flute, cinematic strings and French horn... and bongos that sound like they're from a 1960s spy show.

Health And Efficiency
from Torino
by Cinerama
2002

One of the things I loved to do with Cinerama was to incorporate samples of sounds, narration and conversation, for example, into the tracks. I used recordings that I made on a MiniDisc recorder. I liked the filmic feel that it added. So I've recorded people talking in restaurants or sounds I've heard walking past a reservoir or the sea. I used a bit of a conversation that I recorded on the London Underground for 'Wow', in fact.

The street recording in 'Health And Efficiency' came during a time when I was in New York City. I think we must have been on tour. I came across a building that was being demolished and I was listening to this bloke speaking nostalgically about the way old stuff was being lost, so I switched the recorder on and surreptitiously taped him. He was just talking on the street about how things didn't last very long any more, and it made me think about how that might apply to relationships.

The lyric has a nice air of melancholy to it but in my opinion the most appealing thing about 'Health And Efficiency' is the huge dynamic shift. It's that classic quiet-loud approach that post-rock bands employ. The Wedding Present used it first on 'Bewitched' from *Bizarro,* but on 'Health And Efficiency' the hugeness is further enhanced with the strings. So it's kind of a cross between post-rock and a film soundtrack but with a pop element thrown in as well. The sound on this track is a long way from both *George Best* and *Va Va Voom,* and I like it all the more for that reason.

'Health And Efficiency' is named after the magazine. The lyric describes how it seemed like a 'dirty' book when we were growing up, even though it was just a naturist publication. I think I found a copy in a jumble sale somewhere when I was a kid. I remember feeling slightly embarrassed but also inevitably fascinated by it at the same time.

'Health And Efficiency' is the central track from Cinerama's third album, *Torino,* which I named after the Ford Gran Torino, the car that Starsky and Hutch used to drive in the 1970s TV show. By the time we were recording *Torino* I had improved at arranging orchestration, but I still found it difficult because I know next to nothing about music theory. To me it just seems almost wilfully complex and archaic; it is not user-friendly at all. There are lots of old-fashioned terms and Italian words that make it feel like it's the writings of a secret society. Cinerama was a steep learning curve for me because I had never done anything like that before. When

I'd first started writing songs it was just me with my guitar and a little tape recorder.

Cinerama still exists today. A couple of years ago we were invited to play at festivals in Spain and Portugal, supplemented by local musicians, and that was hugely enjoyable. And we also play every year at my own festival, *At The Edge Of The Sea.* I started the event following a conversation with the rest of the band in a Little Chef near Wakefield in Yorkshire. We were discussing how it was odd that when you're on tour with a support group you see them every day, you watch their set, you become good friends, then, after the tour, you never see them again. I thought it'd be great to have our own little event to which we could invite back the support bands we liked, together with our other favourite bands. We started it in Brighton – where I now live – in 2009 and we've done it every year since. I'm not exaggerating when I say that it's my favourite day of the year. We've even had ex-Wedding Present members like Shaun Charman, Peter Solowka, Paul Dorrington and Darren Belk play with their new bands.

We put together an informal version of Cinerama to play at the first *At The Edge Of The Sea,* just for fun. Everybody switched instruments. But, over the years, we've taken it more and more seriously and added extra musicians and now it's one of the highlights of the day for me. I really love going back to the original recordings and working out how best to reinterpret them with a new group of players.

It was during the time of *Torino* that Simon obtained a guitar amplifier sponsorship deal for the band. It was with a German company called Fame whose valve amplifiers were made in Poland. Up until then my go-to sound had always come from solid-state HH amplifiers but the Fames had a warmer and fuller sound, so I switched. The only problem was that when they needed servicing the engineers would struggle because they were unfamiliar with the Polish circuitry. In the end I had to get rid of them and now I use Fender valve amplifiers.

ui rock you

1996 2 songs

U
UNI RADIO
3

THE WEDDING PRESENT @ WRAS 12/27/9
atlanta

TDK
D   GLR Session 10

NOWHERE FAST
MELIA FLETCHER

CD#8 TWP Live on BBC
Radio Bristol's "Loaded"

HE CHORUS: Hand at own edge
HE LOST IN LIFE: Like it the way

TDK
D   KVRX + SONGS + INT
AUSTIN TX) 4/18/96

OOI   maxell

THERSIDE OF MIDNIGHT
09 96   07 10 96   60

TDK   BBC Radio 5 Session Stereo
AR60   (Second) 1993

D LENOIR - BLACK SESSION
1992

THE WEDDING PRESENT SESSION
on CNFM

HE WEDDING PRESENT   MAX90
RLD SERVICE SESSION + RADIOS 2nd

TDK THE WEDDING PRESENT + RADIO
SESSION AS BROADCAST 22-1-

NG PRESENT @ MTV L.O.D
3/12/96

TDK   KVRX   4 SONGS + INTE
D   (AUSTIN, TX)   4/18/96

TDK
AR90   RADIO 5 SESSION   Cre
ma

TDK   THE WEDDING PRESENT

In 2004, after releasing three Cinerama albums, the band assembled in Seattle – where I was living at the time – to work on what we thought would be the fourth. It was purely by coincidence that I had ended up being based in the same city as Steve Fisk – who had produced *Watusi* for The Wedding Present a decade before – but it seemed like fate had played into our hands, so I asked him if he wanted to record the new record. The answer was an enthusiastic yes.

A year earlier, there had been a significant moment during the recording of a Cinerama session for John Peel at the BBC studios in Maida Vale. On previous Cinerama sessions we'd been in there with keyboards, string quartets, flautists, trumpeters – the works. But on this occasion we were back to plain old guitars, bass and drums. One of the BBC engineers – Miti Adhikari – said to me, 'David, why are you calling this group Cinerama? It's obviously The Wedding Present.' I told him, possibly rather tetchily, that it was because we were Cinerama and we were playing Cinerama songs. I was really happy with the way it was all going at that time and it kind of felt like The Wedding Present might never exist as a band again. But I did sort of see his point.

When I'd started Cinerama in 1997 I thought it would be something interesting to do while The Wedding Present took a six month break. Almost imperceptibly, however, those six months had become six years and Cinerama had gradually replaced The Wedding Present as my focus. But that day Miti had planted a seed.

So there we were, recording in Seattle, thinking about how the music was becoming more and more like The Wedding Present. There were still the Cinerama-style arrangements, of course, and even at the end of 'Interstate 5' we added an extra bit that was pure 'Morricone' with strings, trumpet, Mellotron choir and vibraphone. But if *Disco Volante* had been halfway between the two bands, and *Torino* had moved us even closer in The Wedding Present's direction, we were beginning to feel that with our new songs we'd completed the journey. I remember that Simon and I were sat in my car outside Steve Fisk's studio, just about to start a day of mixing. I said to him, 'You know, I think we should maybe consider releasing this record as The Wedding Present.' To my surprise he wasn't taken aback by the suggestion. In fact, he immediately agreed. It just felt *that* obvious a decision, I suppose. If we released this new record as a Cinerama LP, Cinerama fans were going to be disappointed because it wasn't quite the pop music they'd previously enjoyed and Wedding Present fans wouldn't hear it because, for them, it would have been just another Cinerama album. I spoke to Terry and a few other people and they were almost unanimously in favour of the idea. And so *Take Fountain* started life as a Cinerama LP but became a Wedding Present LP.

I think 'Interstate 5' is a good example of why we rebranded the album, because it's an unmitigated guitar song. This was one of the tracks from the Fisk sessions that guided us to the decision. Funnily enough, the 'feel' of the arrangement was inspired by a cover of the Spiller song 'Groovejet (If This Ain't Love)' that we'd recorded, as Cinerama, for that fateful Peel session in 2003. I loved the Sophie Ellis-Bextor version but, as usual, we wanted to make our interpretation sound completely different. We slowed it down and made it sparser and darker. It worked well, so when we came to arranging 'Interstate 5', we used a similar technique. It's a good example of how when you're arranging someone else's song you often come up with new ideas that you can feed back into your own writing.

Interstate 5 is a motorway that goes all the way down the west coast of the USA from Canada to Mexico. In the song it's a metaphor for escape, especially given that I wrote the song in Seattle. It's all about moving on. There are actually several references to Seattle on *Take Fountain*, but maybe only Seattleites will spot them. The album title's not a Seattle reference, however. Fountain Avenue is a minor street in Los Angeles between the more well known and more congested Sunset and Santa Monica boulevards. So when Johnny Carson asked Bette Davis for advice on the 'best way for an aspiring actress to get into Hollywood', she said, 'Take Fountain.'

I have kind of a love-hate relationship with the United States. I really enjoy going but I'm always looking forward to coming home if I find myself there for any lengthy period of time. I feel very fortunate that in my job I'm able to come and go like that. Jessica McMillan and I lived in the Queen Anne district of Seattle for about a year and a half. The band at that time was scattered all over the place and we would just come together for rehearsals. The drummer, Kari Paavola, lived in London, Simon was in Cologne and Terry had moved to LA, so it didn't matter where I was based, really. It was a bit different from the first line-up, when we all resided within about 10 minutes' walk of each other.

Once, Jessica and I were visiting some of her relatives in California. They're extremely nice people but very religious. Inevitably, the question came up about what I did for a living, and Jessica wanted to show them the terrific promotional video that Yorkshire filmmaker Tim Middlewick had made for 'Interstate 5'. I think she'd forgotten that some of my lyrics are capable of challenging, shall we say, the more conservative of minds. So it was a tense moment for us both when her aunt had to walk away from the computer, visibly shocked, after she'd witnessed my face yelling directly into camera, 'Sex was all you needed!'

Sometimes, when things aren't going too well, I find myself thinking about the fact that I maybe should have had a different career. Perhaps I'd have been more successful devoting my time somewhere else. I was certainly struggling during the Cinerama days. My savings had gone, and the band was barely surviving because I was basically paying for it all myself. We weren't playing many shows and, when we were, it wouldn't be a massive fee. I felt like I wasn't paying the band members what they deserved. But then, when we went back to being The Wedding Present, suddenly the floodgates opened. All the promoters saw that The Wedding Present 'had returned' and wanted us to play. We did a hundred shows in the year or so after *Take Fountain* came out. It was completely bonkers. We were invited to play at festivals all over Europe. It was obviously great to be able to pay the bills again but it was slightly frustrating that it was all down to a name change. Cinerama had made three great records in my opinion. Records that were able to stand up to anything The Wedding Present had released.

For Simon and I it was a long time since we had last been doing The Wedding Present, so going back to it felt odd. We were playing all the old Wedding Present songs, of course, but it felt different because we were coming out of the Cinerama era. I remember a rehearsal where we had a go at 'Anyone Can Make A Mistake' from *George Best*. It's one of those early Wedding Present songs that is played at breakneck speed. I remember Terry laughing her head off at the sight of Simon and me, sweating profusely, trying to do the ridiculously superfast strumming again after a few years away from it. We also had to find a replacement for Kari – the drummer – who left after we'd recorded *Take Fountain*. He had never liked the idea of changing into The Wedding Present because he felt it was a backwards step. I could see what he meant, of course.

MUSIK

MUSIK

THEWEDDINGPRESENT

THEWEDDINGPRESENT MINI PLUS

THEWEDDINGPRESENT

THE WEDDING PRESENT TAKE FOUNTAIN TONE CD060

THE WEDDING PRESENT EL REY

THE WEDDING PRESENT VALENTINA

THEWEDDINGPRESENT

THEWEDDINGPRESENT GOING, GOING...

THEWEDDINGPRESENT GOING, GOING...

THE WEDDING PRESENT GEORGE BEST 30

ザ・ウェディング・プレゼント／ジョージ・ベスト・30

THE WEDDING PRESENT TOMMY

TOMMY THE WEDDING PRESENT

COOK CD 094

COOK CD 094X

TONE CD 029

TONE CD 037

TONE CD 066

TONE BP 066

TONE CD 074

VJR-3205

LEEDS

THE WEDDING PRESENT STNG! FS 1980-1991

THEWEDDINGPRESENT Hit Parade 1

PD75343

THEWEDDINGPRESENT Hit Parade 1

PD75343

THEWEDDINGPRESENT Hit Parade 2

74321 12775 2

THEWEDDINGPRESENT Hit Parade 2

BP 40302-2

74321138092 - THEWEDDINGPRESENT - hit parade 3

82876 503952 THEWEDDINGPRESENT · the hit parade

THE WEDDING PRESENT SINGLES 1995-97

COOK CD 184

THE WEDDING PRESENT SEARCH FOR PARADISE : SINGLES 2004-5 HPR139

THE WEDDING PRESENT YE YE THE BEST OF THE RCA YEARS

88697211822 SONY BMG

THE WEDDING PRESENT HOW THE WEST WAS WON VIBEBX010

THE WEDDING PRESENT UKRAINSKI VISTUPI V JOHNA PEELA PD 74194

THE WEDDING PRESENT UKRAINIAN JOHN PEEL SESSIONS FRESH CD100

MFO 40305

Don't Take Me Home Until I'm Drunk

from El Rey
by The Wedding Present
2008

13

The title of this song is based on a line that Audrey Hepburn's character, Holly Golightly, uses in the 1961 film *Breakfast at Tiffany's*. It falls into the 'poppy' section of the Wedding Present catalogue, which is why we chose it for a single. Some people have said it sounds more like a Cinerama song.

My main co-writer in The Wedding Present has usually been the guitarist in the band at the time and on this occasion that person was Chris McConville. He had a real knack for coming up with a catchy tune and the interplay between his guitar part and Terry's bass line works especially well on this song. I'm also really fond of the lyric. It tells a sad little tale, but I think it's done quite humorously.

It's on the album *El Rey,* most of which I wrote in Los Angeles. It's quite a difficult city in which to live. It's very expensive for one thing. And the traffic's terrible. But I had this idea that while I was there I'd attend lots of glamorous showbiz parties and, I supposed, get Wedding Present music onto some Hollywood blockbuster film scores as a result. But I'm one of the music world's worst networkers, so that didn't really go to plan. But, as a pleasant by-product, I now have more friends in LA than in any other city in the world. Terry – who still lives there – and I recorded the vocals for *El Rey* in Los Angeles, but everything else was recorded in Chicago by Steve Albini (who also mixed it).

People are always asking me what it's like to work with Albini and I think they expect me to relate shocking tales of him being 'difficult'. I suppose he has a reputation. But in my experience nothing could be further from the truth. We have always had a great time working with him. Admittedly, he doesn't suffer fools but, as long as you know what you want to do and are well prepared for the studio, he can have the band sounding amazing extremely quickly. And it's not rocket science either. It's just all about recording a well-rehearsed band in an acoustically suitable room with appropriate equipment. Most of it is done live to capture the feeling that can only be derived from a group playing together. He never wants to be credited as a producer, though. He sees himself more akin to the BBC engineers who recorded sessions for John Peel in Maida Vale and, as a veteran of many a Peel session myself, that's an approach I can happily work with.

I remember something that shows the way in which Albini works. While we were in Chicago recording *El Rey* I had this idea that I'd like to try to overdub a Mellotron on one of the tracks. I did notice they had one in the studio but, as a 'vintage' keyboard, I know that they're notoriously difficult to record. There's a real skill in just making it sound in tune, for one thing. When I mentioned the idea to Steve he said, 'Well, have you got a part already worked out?' I said, 'No, not really.' 'But you know how to play a Mellotron, right?' 'Well, I had a go on one once.' 'So,' he said, 'you want me to spend ages hauling that thing out, setting up microphones and getting a sound just so that we can record something that will probably be unusable?' 'I suppose that's the long and short of it, yes.' 'Well, fuck that!'

I went to bed feeling a little aggrieved. After all, I was paying for the studio time. But ultimately, I didn't really care. It was just a whim I'd had. The next day, however, we went back to the studio and there was the Mellotron, up and running, expertly wired for sound and ready to be recorded.

The sleeve for *El Rey* was designed by Toby Egelnick using photographs taken by Jessica. The pictures were all taken in Los Angeles to be in keeping with the LA theme of the album, and the cover is a shot of a motel in one of the seedier sections of Sunset Boulevard, just five minutes' walk from the Fountain Avenue referred to in *Take Fountain*. It's very rare for members of the band to be pictured in our album artwork, but I appear in this one, albeit dressed in a white rabbit costume. I also used the same winning Jessica/Toby combination for *Valentina* and *Going, Going...* Jessica sends in the ideas that she thinks will work and Toby does the rest. For *Take Fountain* Toby had used pictures taken around Seattle by Jessica's friend Lincoln Mongillo on a Lomo – an old Russian camera – and I think seeing how Toby skilfully employed those images inspired her to revisit her own background in photography.

We have used many different sleeve designers over the years so there has never been a defining look to our LPs. *Watusi, Mini* and *Saturnalia* were all put together by John Underwood, who was a friend of Simon Smith, the drummer on those albums. A couple of the Cinerama records, *Va Va Voom* and *Disco Volante,* were done by Andrew Swainson at Cactus, who was asked to follow my brief of a more 'retro' or 'pop art' feel. Designers Republic in Sheffield came up with the iconic squiggle design for *Bizarro* after we'd been impressed by the sleeves they'd done for our friends Age Of Chance, another Leeds band. It was literally the last concept they showed us after we'd rejected all their earlier ideas during the meeting we had with them.

A graphic artist called Jonathan 'Hitch' Hitchen created many of our other early sleeves. Just after 'Go Out And Get 'Em, Boy!' had been released, Hitch had sent us a postcard he'd designed, illustrating the phrase 'three chords that shook the world', which we liked a lot. He went on to do *Seamonsters* amongst other things but I remember him being particularly pleased when a poster featuring the artwork he'd done for our *Ukrainian John Peel Sessions* mini-LP was seen in Albert Square during an episode of *EastEnders*. Keith and I kind of did the artwork for *George Best* by ourselves, but that was completely steered by and centred on the evocative photograph we'd found of George playing for Manchester United against Coventry City at Highfield Road in 1972. Emboldened by the success of that we decided to have a go at designing the sleeve for the next release, too. It was to be an early singles compilation called *Tommy*. We wasted a ridiculous amount of time, energy and money on that before we got on the phone to the substantially more talented Hitch and begged him to take over.

Deer Caught In The
Headlights

from Valentina
by The Wedding Present
2012

We recorded *Valentina* – which is named after a Guido Crepax comic book character – at a studio in France that had been recommended to us by Albini. Steve had said, 'There are only two studios I'd ever use in Europe. Abbey Road and Black Box'. The latter had been set up by an English engineer called Iain Burgess who had been something of a mentor to Albini. Iain had been responsible for helping to define the hugely influential Chicago sound of the 1980s and early 1990s, a scene from which bands like Albini's own Big Black had emerged. Sadly, we never got to work with Iain because he passed away in 2010, just over a year before we arrived to record *Valentina*.

To mix the album we used a Los Angeles-based producer/ engineer called Andrew Scheps. I think his forte – which you can hear on this track – is that literally everything sounds loud: the guitars, the bass, the drums, the vocals. Everything. In the old days we'd turn the guitars up but that would mean the drums were drowned out or you'd lose the singing. Andrew has this remarkable ability to balance everything so that that somehow just doesn't happen.

I don't really know much about producers to be honest, but our live sound engineer for North American tours, Pete Magdaleno, suggested Andrew when we were looking for someone to mix the Black Box sessions. I think they frequented the same pub in Los Angeles or something. Anyway, Pete said that Andrew was a Wedding Present fan, but I'd never heard of him. So I mentioned it to Graeme Ramsay, who had recently become the Wedding Present guitarist after playing drums on *El Rey*. He thought I was joking. He said, 'Andrew Scheps mixing The Wedding Present? Have you any idea how great that would be?' So I looked up Andrew on Google and saw this ridiculous list of the artists he'd worked with. It was everything from Black Sabbath to Adele. He was this multi-award-winning producer, so I thought I should probably bite his hand off if he wanted to mix our tracks.

By chance, he was over in England. I think Red Hot Chili Peppers had flown him over specifically to mix a live thing they were doing for TV, that's how much he was sought after. So we invited him down to Brighton to sit in on one of our rehearsals. We immediately got on with him really well. The Wedding Present have never really previously been 'produced', as such. Albini and Fisk would certainly not volunteer opinions on tracks unless you specifically asked them, because they don't think it's their place to do so. That was actually why we'd fallen out with our first producer, Chris Allison, during the *George Best* recording sessions. Rightly or wrongly, we have never been happy being told what to do with our songs. But Andrew was much more subtle. And he has such a great ear. So we played through the arrangements in the rehearsal room and he'd make a little suggestion here, a little suggestion there. He just seemed to know how everything should fit together. He didn't comment on every song; he probably only suggested changes to half a dozen or so out of the 20 we played. But when he did recommend something it just worked. It might have been asking Pepe le Moko to change one note on the bass or Charlie Layton to play a drum fill in a slightly different way, but each time we'd play the song again and we'd all agree that it sounded tighter as a result. After that experience, I suppose I could see why people use producers. I suppose it's just a matter of finding the right person for the job.

Even though she had been the bassist (before Pepe had replaced her) it was Terry who came up with the main guitar riff for 'Deer Caught In The Headlights'. She also came up with the bass line and some vocal parts (as she usually did). So this is a total Gedge/de Castro collaboration. I remember that when we started working with her riff it sounded quite poppy but it changed once we'd sorted out the arrangement. Terry told me that 'Can't You Hear Me Knocking' by The Rolling Stones had inspired her while we were working on the rhythm section parts. It's odd, though, how what started out being quite a mellow song became one of the loudest, most intense Wedding Present tracks ever. The end section is absolutely massive.

On the album there's an extra little bit added on to the end of the track, which is me recording Graeme playing the guitar part on an old pump organ. It wasn't part of the studio equipment or anything; it was actually outside, leaning against a wall. I think they were probably getting rid of it. The clattering is me falling over some detritus as I was trying to record him.

The lyric comes from the idea of being startled or shocked by a relationship. Embarrassingly, I had to change the words after we'd played it live a few times after noticing that one of the lines was grammatically incorrect. I used to sing, 'If I was a painter, I'd just paint portraits of you' in the quiet middle bit of the song until someone pointed out that it should be 'were a painter'.

It's always one of our favourite songs to play live because it's a real rocker. It's aggressive and loud. It always goes down well even if people don't know it and, after concerts, I invariably get asked what it was called.

The *Valentina* album story has something of a footnote in that in 2014 I re-recorded the entire LP as Cinerama. The songs were completely re-imagined and arranged by a legendary Spanish musician and producer called Pedro Vigil and then I flew over to his home in Asturias to record the new version with local musicians. It was some of the most fun I've ever had recording an album, and that was partly because it was liberating to give the reins over to someone else. It had been an ambition of mine for some years to re-do a Wedding Present album as Cinerama and I'll be forever grateful to Pedro for helping me make it happen. He replaced all the overdriven guitars with strings, brass and vintage keyboards. We made the end section of the Cinerama version of 'Deer Caught In The Headlights' big, too, but the new version also has a false ending fade out that was inspired by Elvis Presley's 'Suspicious Minds'.

THE WEDDING PRESENT VALENTINA

SNAPSHOTS: STORIES INSPIRED BY WEDDING PRESE

THE WEDDING

WEDDING PRESENT Thank Yer,Very Glad

PRESENT

MARK HODKINSON